Unearthing The Urban Fox

Unearthing The Urban Fox

A householder's guide to fox deterrence

Trevor Williams
and
John Bryant

Unearthing the Urban Fox

First published in Great Britain by The Fox Project in 2000

Second (revised) edition published 2003

Third (revised) edition published 2012

Fourth (revised) edition published 2023 by

Foxolutions
71-75 Shelton Sreet
London
WC2H 9JQ

© Trevor Williams and John Bryant

Foreword by Chris Packham

Illustrations: Barry Small (www.barrysmall-art.co.uk), Thea Olrog, John Bryant, Andrew Wilson

Cover photograph: Dani Clarke

ISBN 978-0-9569614-0-2

Formatted by www.bookformatting.co.uk

Printed and bound in the European Community.

Contents

The Authors

Trevor Williams became involved with wildlife as a campaigner in 1974, his enthusiasm quickly earning him elected positions with various wildlife protection groups and, during the 1980s, a managerial role with the League Against Cruel Sports. His developing interest in foxes rapidly grew beyond the single issue of bloodsports and, in 1990, he formed The Fox Project, a wildlife charity with a specialist wildlife hospital and information bureau, the latter dedicated to researching and advising local authorities, associated wildlife groups and the general public on fox ecology and behaviour. He has written numerous articles on foxes, regularly appears on radio and TV, and presently heads a 150-strong team of professionals and volunteers.

John Bryant was a campaigner for animal rights and wildlife protection for 40 years both voluntarily and professionally. He was an elected member of the RSPCA's Council and had been chairman of Animal Aid's Council, manager of the Ferne Animal Sanctuary, a chief officer of the League Against Cruel Sports, and a founder member of Protect Our Wild Animals (POWA). He also acted as an adviser to members of Parliament involved in piloting wildlife protection laws through Parliament. In 1998 the Fox Project invited him to undertake their pioneering fox deterrence work, he then extended his 'Humane Urban Wildlife Deterrence' service to include other urban animals such as grey squirrels, rats, mice and pigeons in order to enable local authorities, hospitals, property developers, sports clubs, schools, gardeners and private householders to resolve their problems without resorting to the cruel and lethal methods employed by most 'pest control' operators. His previous books include Fettered Kingdoms (1982), Animal Sanctuary (1999) and Living with Urban Wildlife (2002).

Foreword

Tiger, fox , fox, tiger . . . no contest! Both are exquisitely beautiful mammals, both predators, one striped in black, white and rich orange, and the other thick russet red delicately marked with a wonderful symmetry of ebony and ivory shapes.

Both are poster stars, or t-shirt animals as I call them. But there is one very significant difference when it comes to deciding my favourite – I live with foxes, I share my space with them, they are an intrinsic part of my community and, frankly, they are more relevant to me. So foxes have it - Top of my UK Mammal Pops, with perhaps only pine martens nipping at their heels.

So yes, I like them, I even had them as highly unsuitable 'pets' when I was a child, and no, I am obviously not a fence sitter when it comes to foxhunting. That said, I am a pragmatist. I know and understand that my liking is frequently contrasted by others loathing and that whilst, for me, these wonderful animals are a consistent source of joy, for others, they can be a 'nuisance'.

And I firmly believe that for conservation to have any sort of sustainable future we have to suppress our worthiness and realise that we have to put people first, and this means accepting that, for some, foxes are just not gorgeous pin-ups.

That's why this book is such a triumph. It is an honest,

accurate, well-researched and practical guide to living with foxes from both points of view. It entirely embraces a modern, realistic maturity, written by authors with a wealth of experience and the intelligence to see that this is the best use of their knowledge and skills to effect a better life for Britain's foxes. If only this approach were applied more widely; seals/salmon, hen harriers/grouse, peregrines/pigeons . . .

A little while ago I watched one of the most grotesque pieces of television I've ever seen, quite an accomplishment given the levels of unpleasantness we are often exposed to. It involved urban fox 'control' and culminated with a vile, gratuitous and sensationalist execution of a pair of foxes which dragged a normally credible series into an ugly mire of TV trash. I was ashamed that it was aired, not because I'm a softy, nor because I thinks the events mattered in the grand scheme of things, not even because of its tabloid mediocrity, but simply because the whole unpleasant catalogue of events was fuelled by total and utter ignorance. It seriously made me feel that the last twenty years of my life, all the time I've spent trying to better inform people about the lives and habits of other animals, had been a complete waste of time.

Well, here, in your hands, is the essential antidote to that ignorance and, as such, I believe a valuable update to a volume which should continue to educate everyone who shares their space with urban foxes. And if just one episode such as that shameful scenario outlined above is avoided, then its authors can claim to have orchestrated a great success.

Chris Packham

Introduction

This book is not about man's traditional relationship with the fox in rural Britain. Instead, it deals with 21st century fox's colonisation of urban and suburban environments where the nature of problems, both real and imagined, is less complex.

Most urban and suburban fox problems involve fouling, damage to plants or actual or potential residence. Concern may also centre on the perceived threat to man and his pets by disease or aggression.

Before embarking on any action to counter the presence of unwelcome foxes it is important to realise that urban and suburban foxes are neither a new nor a temporary phenomenon. They are here to stay as surely as the squirrel, the pigeon and the starling, all of which species were once exclusively rural. There is nothing unnatural about this. If an environment is attractive and can sustain life it will attract life, a rule which holds equally for all species - man, mouse or magpie.

The Fox Project is the UK's foremost information and advice bureau on foxes. It is part of a charitable trust that incorporates a wildlife rescue and rehabilitation service as well as a fox deterrence consultancy. It may be tempting to consider the two aspects are incompatible. They are not.

Understanding wildlife behaviour by means of close contact

through the rescue facility adds to knowledge that can be made available to householders suffering with unwelcome foxes. In turn, wildlife benefits by the encouragement of humane and effective deterrence methods in preference to the cruel and pointless destruction of yesteryear. At the end of the day, man benefits by greater understanding of the animals that co-own his chosen environment.

The Fox Project is, of course, a pro-fox organisation. If that disturbs you, ask yourself whether someone who dislikes foxes, or who has no interest in their biology and ecology (i.e. 'pest controllers' and foxhunters), is better qualified to advise on fox behaviour. It is unlikely the logic will escape you.

Having developed no proprietary repellents of its own, The Fox Project researched existing brands and adapted their use to knowledge of fox behaviour and field craft that few, if any, product manufacturers enjoy. During the past seventeen years, most UK local authorities have abandoned fox destruction in favour of The Fox Project's methods, and most of Britain's councils regularly refer complainants to its "Fox Deterrence Helpline".

The information provided on the 'Helpline' is necessarily brief and very general. Nonetheless, appreciative response indicates that it conveys sufficient advice to assist many callers in DIY deterrence. Some people will prefer the on-site consultancy service, which is the most comprehensive option, allowing the consultant to see the full picture and to deal with the problem on the client's behalf.

One drawback to on-site service is that it may be beyond the means of some callers. Yet, with the best will in the world, the recorded 'Helpline' cannot cover every possible scenario. No two problems are ever the same. Some folk naturally want more detailed information without the expense of on-site service. But callers cannot hope to convey the details, geography and contours of their property by telephone to someone who is then expected to advise on a situation which he or she can only see in their mind's eye. It's like phoning a plumber and expecting blind advice on how you can fix a leak. How could he know? Nevertheless, there are plumbing manuals and, while none will cover every conceivable situation, they can be useful. This book is intended as a 'plumbing manual', produced in the hope that you can adapt set piece deterrence methods to your particular problems and to solve them without the cost of calling out a wildlife consultant, or (heaven forbid) a 'pest controller'.

Trevor Williams

What's Going On Out There?

You don't have to like foxes to read this chapter, but you should take the view that one must 'know your enemy' if one is to defeat him. Whatever foxes are doing in, or to, your garden, there will be a reason.

The reason may be associated with the season of the year, the age of the animals, their number or their condition. It can depend on whether you keep rabbits, own a dog or cat, if you feed the birds, maintain a fishpond or a swimming pool. Do you back onto a railway line? Is your garden open and flat or uncultivated, with an impenetrable bramble patch?

These are all valid questions and ones that you may have to take into account if you are to understand what's going on and how you can make it stop.

Unless they reside in a dangerous habitat, foxes are fairly predictable creatures, settling for routine as mundane as that of human commuters. This will be apparent to anyone who has sought to attract foxes to their gardens, and who have found the foxes always arrive ten minutes before the food goes out. Put the food out ten minutes sooner and the fox will turn up that much earlier the following day!

We have watched the same social group of foxes criss-crossing each other's paths at the same time every night, each one heading in turn for a known feeding station provided by a fox-friendly householder. We are aware of a nightly ambush of a dog fox who can never get down a narrow alley without being attacked and swatted vigorously by a cat who clearly knows what time he is due. You can set your watch by the sight of a little dog fox called Colin (so christened by the neighbours), and a fat white anonymous cat, who share an evening round where they are fed together by neighbours.

But these are very visible encounters, in some cases dictated by certainty of a meal, and, even in the case of the swatted fox (unless he is just thick!), by the apparent urgent need to get somewhere on time. There is less need for foxes to use the same routes repeatedly when moving around their territories. Yet in most cases that is precisely what they do.

As an example, a studied suburban area of South East London was found to contain an average fox territory of around eighty gardens. The gardens approximate to 40m x 12m and back onto one another on long streets. Some are overgrown and untended, some well stocked with shrubs and deep flowerbeds, even, on occasion, with little woodlands and dingly dells. Others are ruthlessly shorn from panel fence to panel fence, leaving only a two-tone fitted carpet of shiny, striped lawn.

Some gardens contain ponds, swimming pools, birdbaths, bird tables, barbecues, sheds, summerhouses and old air raid shelters. Some lead onto railway lines, parks and allotments. While some of the local roads are busy, most are quiet.

This is fox country, and close examination of any garden in the area will confirm the fact. Visible 'runs' lead from the base of hedges, across lawns, towards ponds or swimming pools and out again. Scoops show an animal has dug a shallow tunnel under the fence. Paw prints and claw marks show where it goes over, for even though the fence is 2m high, a fox can easily 'cat-bounce' over this, hitting the panel half way up and using momentum to reach the top. On the other side, the soil is impacted where paws land heavily and regularly.

A broken ranch fence provides enough room for a fox to pass, but its splintery edge has caught fur too coarse to be that of a cat. The ivy on top of the brick wall is flattened and worn at one point where regular transit has never allowed it to grow. There is a gap between railings where grease from the coat of a passing animal has discoloured the inside edges of two adjacent struts at ground level.

Interesting! If a fox can cross a fence at any point, why does it choose always to use the same place? The reasons don't matter. For our purpose, it is enough that we can identify a regular route in order to attack it with repellents, and this illustrates the point that it is worth learning something about the animal before entering into battle.

The needs of a fox are minimal - a food supply, a water source, privacy and security. A desirable territory must contain all of these. It does not have to be large. In fact, providing it yields all the animal needs, the smaller the better. That way one does not have to spend so much time patrolling and defending it against other foxes. Overcrowding is unacceptable.

I hope, by now, you are beginning to understand how your garden fits into the scheme of things. Perhaps you have realised it is a watering hole. Maybe the impenetrable bramble patch has been the problem all along. It could be you are simply part of a through route and it might be advisable to repair those holes in the fence.

If you are still unsure, add your own recent observations of foxes and consider the time of year. Perhaps your problems are seasonal rather than permanent.

In a book of this size, we could never hope to cover all aspects of 'a year in the life of a fox'. However, it may be useful for you to have some idea of what your 'enemy' is doing at given points of the year. Let's begin with Christmas.

The fox-breeding season begins around mid-December. A courting dog fox will shadow his chosen vixen closely, possibly for several weeks, before she comes into season. During this period, she may be involved in digging and preparing several potential breeding earths, and this is a time when fresh digging may appear at favoured sites such as beneath garden sheds or in grass or soil banks.

A good deal of nocturnal noise will be heard at this time, communications being of major importance to both foxes if they are to be together when the vixen comes into oestrus. This lasts for only three days, during which the pair will mate repeatedly, sometimes locking, or knotting, for some time afterwards - a mechanism designed to maximise the likelihood of conception.

Pregnancies average 53 days, during which time the dog fox will bring food to the vixen, supplementing her own foraging. Some communication calls will still be heard, but less than during the courting season.

After giving birth to her cubs, usually four or five to a litter, the vixen will prefer to stay with them for anything up to ten days, relying, if she can, on the dog fox's offerings. For some reason she seldom allows him to come close to the cubs until they are several weeks old, although few records exist of dog foxes harming their own cubs. In fact, there are many accounts, where vixens have been killed, of the dog fox taking over feeding duties.

The cubs, born blind, open their eyes at around fourteen days. The vixen may now decide to move them to an alternative site, perhaps one that has more room for the youngsters to move around underground. This might account for the sudden onslaught of squeaking and whimpering under your shed, but you may not know for sure for another week or two when the cubs take their first wobbly steps outside.

By now the vixen has resumed her own foraging, although the dutiful dog fox will still be providing for all he is worth. The cubs may be left unattended at the earth during these jaunts, but either parent will round them up and take them back into the earth on their return.

It is now around mid April, and both adults may be looking somewhat scrawny, their appearance made the worse by onset of the annual moult. This is sometimes mistaken for sarcoptic mange. Most vixens will have moved out from the breeding earth by now, tired of the boisterous cubs and their constant, unnecessary demands to be suckled.

More forward cubs may have become quite adventurous, jinking and rolling around the lawn with little regard for human audience. By night, this play may be noticeably noisy, as scraps over pecking order become more serious.

As the cubs develop, the amount of fouling naturally increases. Including the parents, as many as seven animals might be defecating on your lawn nightly. Foodstuffs not required for eating but suitable as playthings will be dragged about and split asunder.

Digging has been added to the cubs' repertoire of skills. Shallow scrapes may appear all over your garden. Long-leafed plants such as daffodils and tulips come in for a great deal of abuse, simply because they are good for rolling on, fun to chew, and, for as long as they last, fine hiding places.

By mid-summer, cubs may be living separately, though they are still social and nocturnal squabbling may still be heard. Although self-sufficient to a degree, they will still be glad to receive supplements from their long-suffering parents, but scrapes will be widespread where they have been in search of easy meals, such as insects, grubs and worms.

As we approach autumn, the more adventurous cubs begin to feel the need to go out and find their own territories. Some leave quietly. Others with rather more fuss, and both territorial and fright-fouling make up more than the usual complement of messages on the lawn.

This must be the most noisy point of the year, when growing siblings, finding food resources are not going as far as when they were smaller, argue constantly. Where unwanted cubs show no sign of leaving home, the parents, particularly the vixen, may join the battle, demanding their territory back.

Foxes are excellent parents, but life goes on and kids should never outstay their welcome!

The result may be disturbed sleep for neighbouring man, but, once begun, dispersal is soon over, and things quieten down again. Territories are now in a state of some flux and trespass is seldom met with much aggression. By October, it is hard to tell some of this year's cubs from full adults as their coats thicken up for winter.

And, following the relatively quiet month of November, it is another Merry Christmas, and another mating season.

About The Urban Fox

As opportunists, foxes will eat almost anything and will usually take the easy option. Despite myth and legend about foxes living entirely at the expense of farmers, they seldom take livestock, a fact which is supported by the Department for Environment, Food and Rural Affairs (DEFRA), which describes fox predation on livestock as 'insignificant'.

A fox's prey consists largely of rodents, rabbits and birds. Any fox, whether rural, urban or suburban, will consume large quantities of earthworms, beetles and other forms of insectivore and invertebrate prey. Seasonally, they will take advantage of fallen apples, pears and cherries, even picking their own blackberries. Carrion, whether dead of natural causes in a country hedge or flattened on a suburban dual carriageway, is always welcome.

Foxes have no particular allegiance to open countryside, and have long been attracted to human habitat, where our untidy habits cause waste and discarded food to be readily available. It is supposed that more than half Britain's households put food out for the birds. Foxes enjoy eating peanuts and fat. They are not averse to bread and will take advantage of fallen food from bird tables. Some people feed their dogs and cats outdoors. Sometimes the fox gets there first!

More direct assistance comes from a growing army of

wildlife friendly householders. It is doubtful a street exists in Britain today where at least one resident does not feed foxes for the sheer pleasure of seeing them around.

In addition to the easy pickings, built-up areas offer surprisingly good habitat. Our railway system provides convenient wildlife corridors through every city. It allows foxes, badgers and muntjac deer to move into the very heart of town. From there, it is a small step to set up home in an overgrown garden, beneath a tool-shed or in one of the many pockets of natural land which, thankfully, still remain in a country so badly scarred by mad bypass disease and concrete-itis.

Colonisation of our cities by foxes is perfectly natural. It is also irreversible. Nature alone decides who can make a living, and where. Man may think he runs the show, but all he can do is find a way to live with it, and to understand it. Indignation won't change anything. Statements such as 'they don't belong in our towns' are meaningless, especially when followed by 'they should be trapped and put back in the country'.

'Putting them back in the country' ignores the fact they were never there in the first place. London, for instance, has been host to foxes for many years. No-one knows exactly how many there are, but some observers believe the population peaked in the late 1960s and has since remained broadly stable. This will be argued by those who say; "So why do I see more of them?" The probable answer is that people are more wildlife friendly today. With fewer hands turned against foxes, they have become less nervous and more tolerant of man. They have simply become more visible.

The best current estimate of London's fox population may be gleaned by extrapolating figures contained in research carried out by Professor Stephen Harris of Bristol University,

Britain's foremost authority on foxes. His figures suggest a population that peaks at 10,000 (following the annual breeding season) and which probably drops below 5,000 (by end of year) in the area contained within the M25 motorway.

This population is not made up of rural 'refugees', as some people imagine. It is indigenous. These are born and bred, street-wise Londoners, who have little or no concept of country life.

The mechanics of trapping and removing foxes on a scale that would have any effect in reducing London's fox population would require hundreds of people who understood fox behaviour, plus hundreds of cage traps. Add transport, holding pens, communications, equipment and research and collation of people who might co-operate in releasing the animals on their land ... well, let's just stop there and examine a previous failed attempt - and a cheaper one at that.

Until around 1989, London Borough of Bromley had a policy of fox 'control'. Their chosen methods of destruction included cage trapping and shooting and the use of terriers. They believed they could reduce the number of foxes in the borough, but, like every other authority that has fallen for this notion, they soon saw the error of their ways.

Despite their best efforts, Bromley's fox population remained the same, year in, year out. Ten years earlier, the London Borough of Lewisham had experienced the same failure to reduce the fox population, despite contracting a team of enthusiastic terrier-men for the purpose. Neighbouring London Boroughs of Lambeth and Southwark had a policy of non-interference with their fox populations yet, interestingly, their fox populations remained the same from one year to the next.

What finally changed Bromley Council's policy was the

discovery, on coming to cost the 'control' scheme, that each dead fox had cost £1500 – that's £4000 at today's prices, and hardly a justifiable use of council funds. Since changing their policy it is interesting to note that the fox population in Bromley has fluctuated only marginally.

So how can that be? Surely wild species overpopulate without 'control'? Not so! Despite the absence of a predator, the world wasn't knee deep in rhinos prior to the appearance of humans!

Foxes have never been controlled by man. The only justification for the continuation of foxhunting was 'control', but if hunting really controlled foxes, bloodsporters would have made themselves redundant many decades before the Hunting Act intervened.

In fact, where destruction occurs on a large scale, it appears an unnaturally high population of foxes will often be present. Strange? Not at all. Foxes are territorial animals. Although not pack animals (they have no concept of co-operation when it comes to hunting or sharing unless cubs are involved) they are highly social. They will tolerate common use of territories up to a point, but this must be dependent on the establishment of a hierarchy, or pecking order. When everyone knows who is who, who is dominant and who is subordinate, everyone is comfortable because everyone knows his or her place in society.

This is particularly relevant as the breeding season approaches. It will be the dominant vixen that will ultimately mate. Not all vixens will do so because subordinate animals will be harried by their superiors, preventing lower ranking vixens from coming into season. This ensures over-population does not occur, for predators are not keen to create unnecessary competition for themselves where food and habitat availability are limited.

In foxhunting areas, there was never a shortage of foxes. This was not only because some hunters preserved and encouraged foxes by providing artificial earths, or even food. Research suggests it was also due to constant culling to a point where the establishment of a stable hierarchy was prevented, where no-one knew who was dominant or subordinate and where no one prevented anyone else from breeding. Hence, destruction is likely to result in a higher, and not a lower population. And you thought foxhunters were there to keep foxes down? Quite the contrary!

By and large, and left to their own devices, foxes appear to control their own population levels, replacing their dead with a similar number of cubs and failing to breed where an optimum population already exists.

Destruction achieves nothing, and destruction methods available for use in urban areas are few. Gassing and poisoning foxes are both illegal, and prosecution for the latter offence is vigorously enforced by the Department for Environment, Food and Rural Affairs (DEFRA).

Shooting is also illegal in most situations, and police have been alerted on many occasions to gunshots and shooting near domestic residencies, sports facilities and allotments, a reasonable enough precaution in these unpredictable times.

Most snares are outlawed today, though one type remains legal. Given the inherent cruelty in snares, some of us have no hesitation in removing and destroying any we may come across on the basis that even the courts sometimes find it impossible to tell the difference between legal and illegal snares. We make no apology for our anger against these indiscriminate contraptions which often claim badgers and domestic pets, and, whenever possible, we will always seek to prosecute those who set them. We would hope, even if a not-so-fox-friendly-person, the reader would never consider such an inhumane option.

Trapping and relocation on a wholesale level is not viable on economic and practical grounds, and, if carried out by cowboy 'pest controllers', may also breach the Abandonment of Animals Act 1960. Under this act, it is illegal to place an animal in a situation where you have reason to believe it might not survive (i.e. irresponsibly removing an urban animal to a rural environment).

That does not mean, given a problem with a specific animal who has learned a particular form of anti-social behaviour, that controlled cage-trapping and relocation by a bona fide wildlife rescue service might not be the answer in some cases. Certainly, The Fox Project has undertaken such cases, although rare, and can recommend other bodies that operate under the same codes of conduct.

There are numerous, non-destructive options for dealing with fox problems. Some appear mildly eccentric, but seem to work anyway. Some years ago, while we were treating a bowling green with repellents following the appearance of shallow scrapes, an Australian member of the bowling club told us he was carrying out his own treatment as well. This, he explained, entailed placing a number of large plastic bottles, filled with water, on the green by night. It was, he said, a system used back home to keep dingos away - and it worked. Intrigued, we asked how it worked. 'Light refraction!' he said, 'They don't like it!'

Our joint treatments worked but we'll never know whether it was the repellents or the bottles that did the trick. Regardless, following local media attention on the issue, an entrepreneurial estate agent invented a perspex dog called 'Getoutofitz', which he marketed with great success on the same principle.

Another option for deterring foxes, though not one suitable for most urban or suburban dwellers was the introduction of a llama into a sheep farmer's flock. Apparently, the possessive llama regarded the flock of sheep as its own property. Llamas can spit a long way, and accurately, too. Any fox that approached the herd would be driven away by a jet of grassy saliva from the belligerent pseudo-sheep.

Less eccentric is the introduction of ultrasonic alarms. The pitch of these is so high that only canines can hear them, but despite a growing number of available brands, our own field tests continue to indicate mixed results.

Not at all eccentric is a form of electric netting we have been recommending for many years. Supplied by a company called 'Foxolutions', the product is versatile, portable and comparatively cheap, and has been used successfully in many varied situations. Where repellents are not effective, as may be the case when defending caged birds or pet rabbits, positive feedback from clients indicate the system is a useful option.

Let us state categorically that nothing you can do, short of building a fortress, will create a permanently fox free zone. If you live within a fox territory, and most people do, you can expect to be used at some time or another as a 'through route'. If that is unacceptable, no-one can help you, not us, not foxhunters, not terrier-men, not 'pest controllers'. You may as well try to stop birds flying over your garden. What you can do is prevent dwelling or dallying on your premises, or at the very least, minimise fox activity on your particular part of the fox's territory, and, in our experience, that is best achieved by use of repellents.

Damage and Nuisance

In rural situations, realistic farmers, who recognise nature's burglars as a permanent potential threat, will defend livestock with secure pens or electric fencing. Such foresight prevents costly losses that might otherwise be incurred by foxes, badgers, otters, stoats, weasels, rats, owls, raptors and a whole range of natural predators. It is clearly more intelligent to think this way than simply to take a gun or a pack of dogs to any real or imagined perpetrator after the livestock is lost.

In urban or suburban gardens the problem is much simpler. For a start, most fox nuisance consists of digging in flowerbeds or lawns, fouling, scent marking, or creating an earth under a garden shed. It seldom involves livestock, but, where it does, or where family pets such as guinea pigs and rabbits are concerned, secure pens, hutches and runs are often the answer. In some cases, electric net fencing may be a more useful solution. Remember the farmer with foresight? It's the same principle. If a predator takes its natural prey (and rabbits are, of course, natural prey to a fox) it's your fault unless you've taken every possible precaution.

For the majority of urban and suburban fox problems the answer must be to attack the territory rather than the animal. Look for the cause behind the symptom. If problems are constant, there has to be a reason the fox is attracted to your property. If you destroy or remove the animal, you must bear in mind you have created a vacant territory. Something about your property attracted the first fox. It will attract another.

London has a peak population of 10,000 foxes. Territories across London are shoulder to shoulder. Whenever a territory falls vacant it will quickly become apparent to other foxes. 'Old Ted's vanished. So has his scent mark. I've always fancied his territory.'

Killing or removing urban or suburban foxes as a means of reducing the population is like trying to fill a bucket full of holes. Don't even think you can do it, and don't let 'pest controllers' allow you to think they can do it, either. Think about your property as potential fox territory. What attracts them? Is it heavy undergrowth? A pond (everyone needs an oasis)? Food left out for pets or for birds? Visible, or free range pet rabbits or guinea pigs? An open shed or summerhouse? Can you remove the attraction?

If you cannot directly remove it, you can certainly disguise or foul the attraction with repellents. But, leaving aside, for the moment, any suggestions for altering structural garden features, let us look at the most common areas of nuisance in urban and suburban gardens:

Digging

Either in the form of tunnels into grass banks, flowerbeds and beneath garden sheds; or smaller scrapes in lawns and planters. Most people, on discovering digging, naturally fear the hole that has appeared in the flowerbed is the beginning of a permanent residence. In most cases this is not so. However, where the excavation goes beneath a shed or similar structure, or deep into a bank, it should be regarded with suspicion, for although this may only represent a bolt-hole (emergency hide-out) it may be an 'earth', 'lair' or 'den'. If it is not, then it might soon become so. The time of year may be relevant in that few new excavations intended as homes will be dug between March and October. However, following juvenile dispersal and as we approach the mating season, new holes may well be intended as winter homes and/or breeding earths.

In the London area, up to 75% of foxes opt for the base of garden sheds as earths. As foxes are basically lazy, a short, shallow dig to get beneath a structure with a ready made roof is infinitely preferable to digging a long tunnel into hard chalk. If the shed is raised on cross beams or a plinth it is even better and decking is even better! This will provide plenty of room for growing cubs to spread out without parents having to go to the trouble and worry of moving them when they get to three or four weeks of age.

Most earths, if intended for permanent use, will have a back door. An escape route is an important consideration. The presence, or absence of a back door may tell you something about the animal's intentions.

Most holes never become earths. They are never intended to be. They are 'scrapes' and are at their most apparent during the summer months, usually indicating activity by young cubs. At three or four months of age, cubs, no longer entirely dependent on parents, start to find prey for themselves. This takes the form of earthworms, beetles, cranefly larvae, cockchafer grubs and whatever can be dug out of the ground without great effort. It is common to find such digging around and into rotting tree stumps and roots where woodlice and other invertebrate prey will congregate.

The softer the ground the better. This was never better illustrated than during 1995's blazing summer months, when the ground was dry and rock hard. Throughout this period, well watered sports facilities were more than usually affected by 'scrapes' both because the areas were easier to dig and because the insect or invertebrate prey were attracted up to the cool, damp soil within reach of their predators.

Scrapes may also appear in planters, tubs and plant troughs, and, again, this is probably down to the soil being more easily dug. They are usually a mistake, as they seldom yield the sought after prey. However, there is sometimes another reason for digging.

If a fox finds more food than it immediately needs, it may cache the surplus and return to find it later with a sense of smell that can locate food buried up to 45cm below the surface. Planters seem to offer a favoured caching point and everything from dead frogs to boiled eggs have been found in the disturbed soil. Sometimes, digging occurs on flowerbeds immediately after turning or tilling. Undoubtedly, this is because it is easier to dig than unprepared soil for insect prey. As any gardener knows, cats are also attracted to fresh soil - though for other reasons!

Interestingly, another reason for digging into flowerbeds is that a fox's amazing sense of smell sometimes misreads the signals. Do you use fish, blood or bonemeal fertilisers? Do the scrapes appear in areas where they have been applied - perhaps around the roses? These fertilisers may suggest buried food to a fox, who will dig and find nothing. But by then the damage is done.

It is not unusual to hear of deceased, recently buried pets being exhumed and partly eaten. Remember, the fox is an opportunist with a remarkable sense of smell that can detect buried food to a depth of 45cm. To avoid unpleasant surprises, bury your pet securely, use a repellent to disguise the location and, for a few weeks, place a stone slab or similar barrier on the surface to deter digging into the recently turned soil.

Fouling - on lawns, flowerbeds and hard surfaces

Often as much a territorial marker as a natural function, and frequency and volume may vary depending on the time of year. It should not be particularly noticeable until late spring, when juveniles become active. As a litter of cubs usually comprises five, and both adults may still be in attendance, play areas may be marked copiously. From late summer, when the annual dispersal of family groups begins, fouling may be used as a weapon in territorial competition or to indicate ownership. In either case, fouling may appear repeatedly at the same points. Similar territorial fouling may occur during the mating season, from Christmas to end of January, though this is less common.

Noise - mating season, cubs, dispersal

May be experienced at any time of the year, though it is seldom so intrusive to sleeping people as that heard during the mating season. The cry of the vixen is a shrill scream guaranteed to raise the hairs on the back of your neck! It is usually heard alternating with the short bark of the dog fox. These are communication sounds. 'Where are you?' 'I'm over here, where are you?' By the end of January things have usually quietened down and will stay that way for a while.

From mid-May the sound of squabbling cubs may be heard. This is a chattering, wittering noise, often rising to a screeching crescendo that has people wondering if the cat's being eaten alive! The 'wow-wow-wow' triple bark of a lonely cub queries the whereabouts of a parent or sibling.

Arguably, the worst point of the year for noise is dispersal season - a few weeks somewhere between late July and mid-October when juveniles are falling out and quarrelling over who's to leave and who will be allowed to stay. Parents will also get involved here, scolding, even chasing away their offspring if they are reluctant to go out and find their own territories. The noise usually consists of protracted screeching and is all the worse for our leaving our bedroom windows open on warm summer nights.

In most cases, despite fears for the safety of animals, both domestic or wild, the aggressive screams are no more than that - no-one is getting hurt at all.

Whilst use of repellents can push the noise-makers further away from your house, you will probably still hear them shouting from a hundred yards away and must recognise a level of impotence in dealing with this type of problem. We certainly do!

Theft - clothing, shoes and garden toys

Foxes are always curious about novel items which crop up on their territories. Being four legged jackdaws, they are also quite acquisitive from an early age, albeit quickly losing interest in the thing they so badly wanted a minute ago! We have found countless chewy items in fox earths; rubber bones, pet toys, smelly shoes, wellington boots, gardening gloves, and, on one occasion, a rubber Ninja Turtle!

The chewy aspect of an item is naturally of interest, just as it would be to a domestic puppy. The smelly attraction, often associated with a kid's trainer (the more expensive, the better!), is possibly regarded as a rival scent mark and the item is removed as much for that reason as to be used as a toy. Certainly, the smell of most recovered stolen property has been deliberately neutralised by the distinctive smell of fox scent-marking. The solution is obvious. There is little point bemoaning the loss of a pair of posh sports shoes if you choose to leave them outside at night.

Scent marking - on shrubs, hard surfaces

Once smelled, never forgotten! Scent marking is a vital part of fox life, indicating to all other neighbourhood animals that this land belongs to ME! When your dog lifts its leg at a lamp-post it is following an instinct to leave signposts to all of its kind who pass that way, even though domestication means they no longer need to do so. With foxes, it's the real thing. One way to establish if an earth is being used by a fox is to stick your head down the hole and breathe in. If you choke, it's in use!

Fox scent marking has been described variously as smelling like creosote, blocked drains, tomcats, smoke, gangrene, boiled glue and burned toffee. Take your choice! If scent-marking is causing a problem it is usually because the fox has decided to use a point close to the house, even a corner of the house itself, as a scent-marking point. These points are important and they will be reinforced regularly. Other favoured sites may be physical features such as tree stumps, statues or planters. In some cases, a shrub or low growing plant is marked. Favourites may include dwarf conifers, heather and lavender.

Urinating - on lawns or plants

This is not a particularly common problem, and cats and dogs are more often to blame for brown rings on lawns or plants dying from urine burns. While droplets of urine may be used as a territorial marker in the same way as fouling it is unusual for this to become apparent to the human nose.

Pet predation - rabbits, guinea pigs, tortoises, caged birds, chickens

We have twice heard of tortoises being attacked by foxes, but know of many more situations where no interest is taken in them at all. On the other hand, rabbits, rodents and caged birds are natural prey and it follows that pet housing and aviaries must be secure enough so that, although foxes may continue to 'window shop', they will be unable to gain access to your animals.

Territorial disputes with pets - cats, dogs

Despite media scare stories, there are relatively few documented cases where cats have been attacked and subsequently killed by foxes. In fact, The Fox Project's rescue operation frequently treats cubs and fully adult foxes following attacks by cats, which are both better armed and more aggressive. There is also less difference in their comparative weight and size than many people imagine.

That is not to say foxes never eat cats! The remains of cats have been found at fox earths and occasionally in fox faeces, but every post mortem The Fox Project has commissioned has shown these to be the result of foxes scavenging cats that were either killed on the road or excavated from garden graves.

Reports of 'huge' foxes are always met with wry smiles by naturalists who know the average adult fox weighs in at 5.5kg with a body length of just over 60cm, excluding tail. If you can cope with the idea that an adult fox can get through a 12cm square hole – the size of the average household air-brick - you will have a better idea of the true bulk of a fox and will understand why they tend to treat cats with respect, generally giving them a wide berth.

Whilst foxes seem to regard domestic dogs with contempt, probably with some justification, they will usually take flight rather than fight. If you are a predator and wish to remain successful you do not risk injury and the resultant loss of effectiveness just to make a point! If a territorial dispute arises between a fox and a dog it sometimes results in heavy fouling by the fox - usually in the absence of the dog.

Territorial disputes happen much more frequently between cat and fox. In an urban or suburban area, the territorial ranges of foxes and cats will overlap, but while most ignore each other and others actually become friends, some cats will ambush and attack a fox at every opportunity.

Occasionally, violence is reported during March and early April, when cubs are very small and dependent. Cats and dogs are both given to sticking their heads under sheds where they are not wanted. Sometimes they get bitten by maternal vixens, for the parents of any species will naturally defend their young. These incidents are skirmishes rather than battles, and, given the number of infant cubs killed or savaged by dogs and cats each year, there is undoubted justification for the vixen's concern.

Foxes may be social animals but they are solitary hunters, having no concept of hunting prey as a pack. Consequently, they have no need to seek large and difficult prey and seldom regard anything larger than a rabbit as fair game.

Children - concern about attack or disease

The effect on parents of a story that recently made the press will be felt for years to come. Few naturalists were prepared to believe the story, which involved an attack on two children, sleeping in separate beds. The doubts are based partly on contradictions surrounding the event, the fact the description of the 'attack' flew in the face of scientific knowledge and because no fox experts were given access to investigate. Our own repeated offers to provide free on-site service and deterrence equipment were ignored, as were those of other experts. As such, the story is widely regarded as being not dissimilar to another high-profile incident that occurred in 2002.

In that event, the national press carried an item about a baby having been attacked by a fox. Headlines screamed "Sleeping baby savaged by fox" and "Fox mauled my baby as she slept". The child's father was reported as saying "The fox was dragging her towards the door" and "She was soaked in blood".

On the night of the incident the attending doctor telephoned to ask if there were any specifically fox-related diseases for which he should be looking. We assured him there were none, and asked about the baby's wounds. "Just a tiny mark, hardly enough to draw blood," he replied, adding, "Not that I believe the story, but patient confidentiality prevents me from saying more".

We were naturally intrigued, as no substantiated records existed of anybody in Britain having ever been attacked by a fox – nipped, yes, snarled at, yes, but not *attacked*. And in every case where a bite had been inflicted, the animal was subsequently caught, examined and found to be concussed -

even brain damaged.

One such recent incident showed the animal to be suffering from toxoplasmosis, a cat disease which, if contracted by foxes, causes abnormal behaviour, confusion and a lack of natural caution or fear to the point where what the deranged animal probably intended as a curious nibble becomes an unintentionally nasty bite.

As The Fox Project was not directly involved in the aforementioned baby-biting stories, our opinion is simply that – an opinion. However, Social Services, police and neighbours all telephoned us in the days following the latter incident, unanimously pooh-poohing the story. So did numerous tabloid journalists, who universally doubted the story's veracity. However, tabloid journalists being what tabloid journalists are, those doubts did nothing to curb their instinct for a spot of scare-mongering sensationalism. (Moral: don't believe all you read in the papers!)

Returning to those various sources of information, we were advised another child in the family had been bitten by the family dog a few weeks before and social services had threatened, unless the dog went, that they would take all the children – understood to be seven in number – into care. What we know for certain is that the dog did *not* go until the second child was bitten. A fox was blamed, for which social services were hardly able to hold the parents responsible, and the dog was never seen again.

Regardless of whether the incidents were true or not, they would have to be seen against a background where an average 6,000 postal workers alone are attacked every year in the UK by pet dogs, and where children are frequently killed or maimed by supposedly tame dogs – which rather puts things into perspective.

IF IT'S IN THE
PAPER...IT
MUST BE
TRUE

As to disease, there is little danger from foxes in Britain. The erroneous, but widely held belief that foxes are 'vermin' is at the root of such concern. The notion appears to come primarily from gamekeepers, who seem to regard all things, except for the immigrant pheasant, as vermin. I have an old dictionary that states: "VERMIN, any animal or bird which is a threat to game interests, i.e. foxes, stoats, weasels, badgers and owls." Owls? Need I go on?

The only body officially entitled to classify a creature as 'vermin' is the Department for Environment, Food and Rural Affairs (DEFRA). They do not list the fox as such, and never have, but rural folklore has time-coded the message "foxes are vermin and rats are vermin, rats carry disease so foxes carry disease".

The Fox Project rescue service regularly receives foxes suffering from sarcoptic mange, hepatitis, leptospirosis, pneumonia, meningitis, toxoplasmosis and various parasites. Diseases such as distemper and parvovirus have never been diagnosed in foxes received by the organisation and foxes are not even prone to major flea infestations unless debilitated by other problems.

None of these ailments or parasites are likely to transmit readily, or at all, to man, and although cats and dogs may both be susceptible to some of these problems, it is far from likely a fox would be the agent of transmission without close, if not direct contact. Given the animal's natural timidity, such a level of contact will be rare.

Rescuers working with The Fox Project handle sick foxes daily. They are asking for trouble. It never happens. It would, therefore, be extremely unlucky for someone with only a casual connection with foxes to contract any of these problems.

Since 1906, when rabies died out in the UK, the greatest perceived threat of disease from animals to humans is toxoplasmosis and toxocariasis. Domestic cats and dogs, coming into closer contact with man, and evidently more prone to these diseases, must, therefore, be seen to be a greater threat. Be not alarmed, however, as the risk of serious effects from either disease is so small as to be practically imperceptible.

All things considered, there is no reason our human population cannot share territory with a fox population so long as we are not adversely affected. And for the most part, we're not affected by anything worse than a bit of poo, a hint of scent mark, some disturbed soil, a nocturnal shriek or a missing sports shoe. If we so wish - and as you have read this far, I must assume you *do* so wish – we can deal with these problems easily, logically and humanely. If we *don't* so wish, and our cold response is to call in the assassins, we're not the species I hope we are.

Householders' Guide To Fox Deterrence

Overview

When you come to think of it, most animals, including human beings, are territorial. We humans have our homes and gardens which are strictly reserved for our families and for those we invite in. We take action to prevent others entering our 'space', with locked doors and windows, garden fences, padlocked gates, 'no trespassing – private' signs and alarm systems. We have to share our wider environment - street, village, city, county and country, but we resent unwelcome intruders. As we learn our 'territory' we settle on our favourite routes around it and our favourite places in it - shops, parks, and entertainment centres. We learn the unpleasant places in our territories that we prefer to avoid - dark alleys, busy roads, and areas we might fear for our safety – high streets on a Friday night!

Foxes are no different. In urban areas, to establish a territory large enough to accommodate their basic essentials – food and water, safe dens in which to rear a family, and places where they can rest free from disturbance - a pair of foxes may need to establish a home territory of some 60 to 80 acres – including

200 or more residential gardens. Having mapped out their territory they have to use 'notices' to inform other foxes that it is occupied and if necessary they will defend it with force against take-over bids. They also have to learn about the complexities and unpredictability of humans, some of whom welcome them, some tolerate them, others attack them. They also need to be wary of mans' *best friend* and to learn which cats are hostile and which are not.

Based on a decade of hands-on experience I am confident that virtually all forms of 'fox nuisance' can either be prevented or at the very least mitigated by the adoption of deterrence tactics. These tactics are based on the pioneering work of the Fox Project, formed in 1991, which sought to dispel the high levels of ignorance and mythology spread eagerly by those with vested interests in killing foxes, such as hunters and so-called 'pest controllers'.

Whatever one's views on foxes, the indisputable facts never told to their clients by 'pest controllers' are that killing or removing foxes from a location where they are causing a nuisance, not only involves causing suffering, but also creates a vacant territory for neighbouring foxes to fill – often within days. Capturing and 'relocating' unwelcome foxes sounds good, but is often worse than shooting them, and is at least a technical offence of cruelty under the Abandonment of Animals Act 1960. The practice is thus condemned by the government, the RSPCA and all reputable wildlife groups. Removing them from their territory and dumping them elsewhere subjects them to attack from the existing territory holders, where they don't know where to find food and water, and have no time to learn of local dangers such as busy roads and free-ranging dogs. Thus it should be no surprise that radio-collar tracking research has revealed that foxes rarely survive such 'hard-release' practices. Leaving foxes in their territory to keep other foxes away, letting them get on with their (short) lives, but deterring them from specific locations or activities, is both more humane and logical than killing or 'relocation'.

To illustrate the futility of destruction, in excess of sixty per cent of the fox population dies annually, but is quickly restored in one breeding season. Government and local authority attempts to exterminate foxes from London continued from 1940 into the 80s. The scheme was eventually abandoned because there were more foxes than when the slaughter started, and spread over a wider area. In the countryside much fox mortality is due to unnecessary human persecution with dogs, guns, snares and illegal poisoning, but the urban fox population fares little better. The 'predator' is still man, but the main instrument is the motor-vehicle. Either way a British fox is unlikely to live to see its second birthday (less than a fifth of its possible life-span). It is true that foxes can be a nuisance on occasions, but there is no record of members of the public contracting diseases from foxes and apart from one highly publicised (though unverified) allegation of an 'attack' on twin babies in a bedroom of a Hackney home in the summer of 2010 (an incident described by the government as unprecedented and 'extremely rare') foxes clearly do not go around attacking human beings of any age. Compared with the 5,500 UK citizens hospitalised by dog attacks annually (including children killed by family pets) and the reported 1,000 people hospitalised (including around a dozen deaths) from bee and wasp stings, foxes are not exactly a threat to the survival of mankind! Prior to the Hackney incident, polls showed that 80 per cent of today's city and town dwellers are happy to share their environment with wild foxes. Thousands of people derive great pleasure from watching them and even feeding them - not something I recommend, but which I fully understand. The following advice is mainly for householders who suffer from fox nuisance, suggests the possible causes and offers some humane, intelligent and non-lethal solutions.

Why my garden?

The main complaints about foxes in residential areas, depending on the time of the year, are fouling and 'spraying', bringing in rubbish, digging holes, screaming, damaging garden lighting cables, irrigation systems and play equipment, harassing pets such as rabbits, guinea-pigs and poultry, attempting to get through cat flaps, climbing on cars, setting up home under garden sheds and decking, and even entering underfloor cavities via missing air-vents.

The first step in devising a deterrence programme is to consider what attractions are present.

Neighbouring properties

If you live adjacent to any of the following, you are almost certain to become aware of considerable fox activity. Cemeteries, allotments, sports clubs, hospitals, schools, nursing homes, waste-land, neglected gardens and wildlife reserves. The one thing all such places have in common is an absence of dogs! Urban foxes are not concerned about the presence of humans, as they know that we cannot chase and catch them, but they know that dogs are a very different matter. Even though an adult fox can usually escape from the average dog, they know their cubs are extremely vulnerable. Therefore foxes normally set up their base in a part of their territory to which dogs never or rarely gain access. Clearly if you have such a place adjacent to your home, you are more likely to be visited by foxes, than folk living at the other end of their territory. And there may be aspects of your property that will almost guarantee regular visits from you foxy neighbours.

Repellents

Firstly, a warning about the use of repellents. Whenever complaints about foxes are discussed in an area, some know-it-all will immediately suggest putting down products such as Creosote (now an outlawed product), or mothballs, or Jeyes Fluid. I have even known Council staff to recommend pouring diesel oil in and around fox earths. Using any of these highly toxic products to deter animals is a criminal offence under the Environment Protection Act. If the label of any chemical product or compound does not state that it may be used as an animal repellent, it is an offence to use it in such a way.

Foxes defend territory by warning off other foxes with scent marking, urine and solid droppings. These signs tell any newcomer that the territory is already taken and foxes do not like overpopulation. Fox deterrence simply uses man-made versions of these smells to confuse the animals' instincts and to undermine their control of the territory. Also, when a vixen has young, she will become extremely nervous if a strange scent appears in close proximity and will prefer to move her cubs to somewhere safer as soon as possible. A confused fox is a nervous fox and a nervous fox will prefer to avoid what it does not understand.

There are commercial repellents to suit different conditions. If you want to protect a lawn or particular plants from damage, a product called "Scoot" is very effective. This comes as a powder which is dissolved in water and then sprayed on the foliage or grass you wish to protect using a garden sprayer or watering can.

To defend soil areas such as flower beds or planters, a product called "Get off" is the more appropriate option. "Get off" consists of Citronella scented jelly granules and is particularly useful in dissuading foxes from digging holes. It will also encourage them to abandon established earths or dens or to create new ones. Two treatments over a two week period usually do the trick.

Do not be tempted to block the entrance to any hole unless you are certain it is unoccupied, as this could constitute burying animals alive. Apart from the inhumanity involved, this is also, quite rightly, highly illegal. If you are unsure whether foxes are already resident inside a tunnel or under a shed, a good tip is to bunch up newspaper and stuff it loosely into the tunnel entrance. This will serve as an indicator. If the newspaper stays in place for two nights in a row, then clearly no fox is coming and going. If it bothers you that your actions are making the animals homeless, do not worry. An urban fox will have at least three homes, often many more. This is a species that always has a back-up plan.

"Scoot" and "Get Off" are relatively cheap and are available from most good garden centres and hardware stores. Both are non-toxic and harmless to man, cat, dog and fox alike. As to how long the repellents last, they really do not need to last very long. You are trying to change an animal's habit and upsetting the animal with repellents usually works quickly.

There are also many "ultra-sonic" devices advertised as effective against anything from ants to dogs. Some people have been satisfied that such devices appear to have deterred mice, but personally, I have never found any that effectively deter cats, dogs or foxes. When you consider all the noises created by human beings in an urban area – cars, motorcycles, lawn-mowers, strimmers, radios, sirens, aircraft, fire-works, chain-saws etc, I think foxes just shrug their shoulders when they encounter a new and expensive "anti-fox ultra-sonic" device and do the equivalent of muttering under their breath, "Damn noisy human beings again!" as they pass by going about their business. That said, a recently produced sonic "fox repeller" has impressed the owner of a small timber company in Kent, who had been troubled by foxes fouling on his stored timber, resulting in his staff and customers complaining about getting their hands and clothes soiled when handling the wood. After installing the "repeller" the problem ceased. However, I recommend that anyone tempted to purchase an ultra-sonic pest control device should insist that a "money back guarantee if not delighted" clause comes with the device.

I consider the scent of dogs can be effective as a repellent, particularly their "scent-marking" with urine. I have also used clumps of freshly groomed-out dog hair placed around a den occupied by young cubs to persuade the vixen to move them away from the apparent danger of dogs.

However, if after using repellents in your garden you think you will never see a fox again – forget it! There is no such place as a fox free zone. Repellents simply solve your immediate problem, whether it be garden damage, fouling, or digging and it may or may not recur. There is no way you can create a permanently fox free zone, but if your problem recurs, you now know how to solve it.

If you are in any doubt the softly, softly approach works, a survey carried out on The Fox Project clients at Greenwich University showed they were satisfied with the results achieved by our recommended consultants in well over 95% of cases. You, the DIY practitioner, may not be quite so successful, but after reading the above you now have the same weapons as those our consultants use and even they could do no more without seeing your problem at first hand.

Do not be fooled by old fashioned, so-called pest controllers, who will either kill or relocate the fox, often quite illegally. What they will not tell you as they cheerfully pocket your cash, is that fresh foxes will fill vacant territory within two or three weeks at the most. Bear in mind also that animal protection laws mean poisoning and gassing are illegal, carrying a fine of £5,000 per animal; snares can as easily catch and injure domestic pets, which could get you sued by neighbours and local authorities and the police are rightly concerned about guns being used in urban and suburban areas.

In any event, do you really want to kill something when you do not have to? We doubt if you do. Most people are more humane than that. For moral and legal reasons, deterrence is the best method of fox control. For practical reasons it is far more effective than the more extreme methods and for economical reasons, it is by far the cheapest option.

Fouling

This is probably the single most frequent complaint about urban foxes. It is worth pointing out however, that several times I have been called-out by people complaining about prolific nightly fouling by foxes on their gardens, only to visit and point out to highly embarrassed householders that what they thought were fox droppings all over the lawn, were merely the harmless casts of earthworms! On other occasions the droppings have been left by local cats – not all cats dig holes and bury their faeces! On other occasions what people have described as the offensive stink of fox urine, is in fact the odour from the leaves of certain privet bushes. The 'good' thing about foxes is that they proudly display their droppings to the world. Indeed, it is the equivalent of graffiti 'tags' – a 'this is my patch' notice. It is frequently found on a path, doorstep, on top of a garden ornament or prominent plant. This is typical canine behaviour. If you are a dog walker who takes your dog onto the local park, you will often see a traffic-cone that the local kids have been using as a 'make-do' goal-post or cricket stumps. Every unleashed dog will run to the cone and urinate on it. Adult foxes 'mark' places which are likely to be travelled by other animals, including human beings. The reaction by most people finding a fox dropping on their path or step, is to clear it away and then scrub the spot with bleach or disinfectant. The chances are that the next day there will be another dropping on the same spot. I have found that the most effective way of countering this sort of territorial 'marking' is to pick up the dropping with a plastic bag (poop-scoop bags are best), but don't attempt to scrub out the stain or trace. Instead, 'over-mark' the spot with one or two squirts only of 'Wash & Get Off' anti-fouling repellent. I surmise that when all traces of the previous dropping have disappeared the fox is prompted to repeat the 'notice', but if its nose tells it that its 'notice has been 'over-marked' by a stronger scent, they react as if they are being challenged by some other unknown animal. I have never known a fox repeat foul on or close to a spot marked with 'Wash & Get Off'. Where foxes mark with their urine, (which I can only describe as smelling like a slight tinge of burnt rubber and not particularly offensive) 'Wash & Get Off' again seems to work well.

Ponds

A source of drinking water (and the odd frog or fish) is extremely valuable to a family of foxes. If possible, vixens will always attempt to create a den fairly near to a source of water. Cubs born in walled gardens with no pond or water feature, can suffer from dehydration in the summer until they are old enough to escape and follow their parents further afield. If you really don't want foxes to visit your pond, you could cover it with a two-inch weld-mesh frame fitted high enough above the surface to prevent foxes sticking their tongues through the mesh to lap the water, or you could employ a 'water-squirting' device that detects intruding animals and automatically fires a jet of water to scare them off.

There are two known devices available the 'Scarecrow' and the 'Jet-Spray Repeller'. The former is more expensive, but is the superior machine.

Shrubs and trees

Trees and shrubs provide concealment for wildlife and in many gardens foxes can find a sheltered spot unseen by anyone in which to curl up and sleep. For a wild animal to find a dry, sheltered place to sleep in safety is a real bonus. In parts of London I know well, such lying-up places are often on top of walls or sheds thickly covered in ivy. A row of conifers at the end of the garden means that the soil will be very dry and as well as digging a little 'dish-shaped' bed, foxes often attempt to dig dens ('earths') amongst the root systems. If you don't want foxes setting up home under your conifers, cut back the lower branches to a height of a metre or so to expose the area to view and where there are signs of digging, soak the area with water. Large pampas grass plants need to be checked regularly for signs of foxes creating a secluded lying-up place right in the centre of the bush or digging a den underneath it.

Digging

There are various 'forms' of digging. Foxes will dig for earthworms and grubs such as cock-chafer larva and if there is a severe chafer infestation in your lawn, foxes may make a real mess of it. Water squirting devices (see 'ponds') are the best defence. If you find a large hole that forms the entrance to a tunnel (say 20cm diameter) you should be able to gauge how deep it goes by the amount of soil excavated, or by gently probing with a plastic or wooden rod. If it only goes in a foot or two and is empty, open it up with a spade and back-fill, mixing a repellent such as 'Get Off My Garden' (or human urine) in with the soil you use to fill the hole. You may have to repeat the operation a few times as the fox may return several times to dig out the hole again – just out of curiosity. However, if you keep the soil soaking wet and sloppy the foxes will leave it alone. If you discover a really deep tunnel, and the period is in the first five months of the year, you must proceed with care, because it may be contain a litter of cubs and/or their mother. March is the main month of birth, but the period can be much earlier or later. To check for use lightly crumple up a couple of large sheets of newspaper and lightly wedge them in the entrance. Spray a couple of squirts of 'Wash & Get Off' repellent on the outside surface of the newspaper 'plug' to help deter passing foxes from casually investigating. Any fox inside, or any vixen outside returning to her cubs, can easily move the paper. If the paper remains undisturbed for 48 hours, it is normally safe to assume that no foxes are using the tunnel.

However, I recommend that the tunnel is slowly and carefully excavated with a spade by hand until the length of the tunnel has been exposed (just in case young orphan cubs are at the end of the tunnel) in which case you will need to call a local wildlife rescue group or animal welfare society.

If the tunnel is empty, back-fill, using repellent such as 'Get Off My Garden' as mentioned above, and place a heavy paving slab or pegged-down sheet of weld-mesh over the blocked entrance. Merely blocking is not adequate, as foxes will sense the cavity beyond the entrance, and attempt to open it up again. You may need to keep the entrance area sopping-wet for a few days to deter them digging.

If foxes keep digging in your flower beds, it may be because you have used a fertiliser containing animal products such as blood, bone-meal or poultry manure. Foxes in the wild bury surplus 'kills' or other food, and if their fantastic sense of smell suggests to them that an animal or food is buried in your flower beds, they will dig up huge areas looking for the free meal. If you have used such fertilisers you could try disguising the smell with strong citrus-scented type cat and dog repellents such as 'Get Off My Garden'.

Fences

Foxes often dig gaps under fences simply because it is easier to squeeze under a fence than climb over it. It takes a lot of energy to vault maybe a hundred two-metre high fences during a nightly patrol! The second less obvious reason however, could be that adult foxes are creating holes to enable their cubs which are too young to climb, to start exploring their local environment. Such digging may well be an indication that a vixen has either produced cubs (or intends to) in a den in your, or a neighbour's, garden. Blocking the gap with bricks or soil, usually results either in the hole being dug out again, or in another gap being dug elsewhere in the fence–line. Sometimes it makes sense to leave the foxes a gap under the fence rather than suffer the damage caused by animals scrambling over, but if you wish to block it, the best method is hammering wooden or metal rods into the ground 5 cms apart to form an underground barrier at the foot of the fence, or laying paving slabs or pegged-down rigid sheets of weld-mesh flat on the

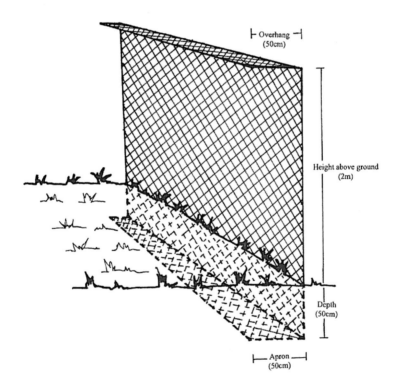

ground along the bottom of the fence line to physically prevent foxes digging under. (see also 'Sheds and Decking').

The most effective wooden fence for reducing fox activity is two metre high closeboard fencing with *vertical* boards. Horizontal boards form useful steps that will help animals climb. Adding another 30cms or more to the effective height of the fence by fixing trellis is often enough to deter foxes, although the holes in the trellis should be no bigger than 8 cms. Police often advise fixing such trellis to the top of fences to deter burglars as the weight of intruders climbing over the trellis often causes it to break noisily.

Special strips of plastic cones called 'prickle strips' can be obtained from garden centres or 'Foxolutions' (see References and Contacts) and fixed to the top of fences to deter animal or human intruders. The points of the cones are sharp enough to be extremely uncomfortable to hands and paws, but will not puncture the skin. I have come across people who have fitted barbed-wire or even strips of carpet-gripper along the tops of the fences in an effort to deter intruding animal or people. This is extremely dangerous as barbed wire and carpet gripper can either impale or lacerate the paws of animals or the fingers of humans. In the case of animals or people being injured by such devices, the householder could find him or herself in receipt of criminal charges and/or civil proceedings for damages. If a domestic animal is injured in this way, the result could be a criminal conviction and heavy fine (even a custodial sentence) under the Animal Welfare Act 2006, and in the case of wild animals, the Wild Mammals (Protection) Act 1996. Wildlife rescuers frequently have to deal with foxes and other animals that have been discovered hanging by a limb from barbed wire. An animal does not have to hang in such a position for very long before the limb is permanently disabled – which usually means destruction and at the very best amputation. Some countries (Germany for one) take this risk to wildlife so seriously, that a government licence is needed for the erection of a barbed wire fence.

In the USA pets are often prevented from escaping over fences, or nuisance wildlife prevented from climbing in, by a device called Coyote Roller, which consists of a revolving metal tube fitted along the top of fences so that an animal attempting to climb the fence will fall back once it gets its front feet on the roller. Keep an eye on the web site of Foxolutions which is continuously searching for new humane deterrence systems worldwide. (See www.foxolutions.co.uk).

If your neighbour wishes to cooperate with you on deterring foxes, you could fix a horizontal 'overhang' at the top of the fences. The overhang needs to protrude 40 cms or so either side so that foxes cannot physically clamber up and over the fence. Foxes can climb a 2 metre high chain-link fence unless an 'overhang' is fixed at the top. Even then they may dig underneath the fence so a similar 'underhang' needs to be pegged along the ground at the bottom of the fence.

In certain situations, such as protecting pets or livestock, or valued crops, plants or lawns, electric fencing will safely deter foxes and other unwanted animal intruders. The Fox Project recommends electric fences and netting supplied by Foxolutions. (See www.foxolutions.co.uk)

Compost heaps

Accessible compost heaps attract foxes. Foxes can dig grubs, worms, and nests of rats and mice out of them, or simply take a nap on top and enjoy the heat rising out of the heap, or if it's a large established compost heap, even dig a den inside it. (See 'digging' for closing down such a den.) Such compost heaps are usually at the far end of the garden, often hidden by shrubs or trees. If you don't want foxes using it, either remove the compost heap altogether, or build a timber and wire-meshed compost box with a lid, or use one of the many plastic enclosed composters supplied by garden centres.

Bird feeding

Another 'high value' facility is bird food, whether it's thrown out on the ground, or placed in hanging feeders or on bird tables. Although, the foxes may take little of the food itself, they are likely to be more interested in the chance to ambush pigeons, squirrels or rats which turn up to scavenge spilt bird food. If you don't want foxes or other scavengers visiting, either stop feeding the birds, or find a way to prevent spilt food reaching the ground.

Fallen fruit

Another major attraction for foxes is fallen fruit. It is not commonly appreciated that foxes are big fruit eaters. Pears and cherries are particular favourites, but blackberries, strawberries, apples and plums are also eaten. Thus, pips and stones can be seen in the fox's droppings. If you don't want foxes visiting, pick up fruit as soon as it falls.

Corner houses

If your house is the end of a terrace or a corner house you may find that foxes often cut across your front garden or climb over the rear fences. I have seen front and back gardens with an obvious groove across the lawns where generations of foxes have travelled. Although foxes commonly roam streets at night and happily trot along the pavement, they don't like going around blind corners and a corner house may have fences or walls that prevent the fox seeing around the corner into the adjoining street. This could be dangerous for a patrolling fox. Someone may be walking their dog late at night, or if the corner is also the edge of the fox's territory there may be a rival neighbour coming the other way. Therefore cutting the corner makes perfect sense and the corner house garden is therefore valuable enough for the fox to mark it with its faeces or urine. Raising the height of your fences in the back garden with trellis may cause the fox to change its route. Front gardens usually have either low walls or fences, or none at all if the estate is 'open plan', and therefore deterrence is difficult. If the foxes are not causing any particular problem in the front garden it may not be worth taking any action. If digging or fouling, or jumping on your car, see other sections in this publication.

Side access

A property is also of high value to foxes if it has a side alley or gap at the side of the house that allows foxes to get to road from the rear gardens. The road may well be the boundary of their territory and it has to be regularly patrolled and 'marked' to deter other foxes from moving in. The houses of the street may be terraced with perhaps just one or two alleyways providing access to the rear of the properties. Foxes will consistently use such routes and regularly mark them with faeces or urine to warn neighbouring foxes to avoid the route. If there is a wooden gate there may be a gap underneath big enough for a fox to squeeze under. Restrict the gap to no more than 8 cms by relocating the hinges or, if the path is soil, placing a paving slab under the gate to prevent foxes digging under the gate. With wrought-iron gates, the foxes can often squeeze through the bars – you may see a dark smear left by their coat on the bars.

Fixing sheets of light weld-mesh to the gate with cable-ties will force foxes to find another route, but remember the gap between the hinge end of the gate and the gate-post, or the gap underneath the gate. Again, action may be needed to restrict these gaps to no more than 8cms.

Rubbish

Foxes will always be attracted to dustbins or rubbish bags left outside. Wheelie-bins defeat foxes, but if your local authority is still living in the nineteenth century and has a policy of relying on 'black plastic bags', the full bags should be stored in a fox (and rodent) proof structure. Some housing estates have brick-built compounds in which rubbish bins are stored. Many of them have no roof, and the doors have a large gap at the bottom. Foxes, local cats and other scavengers can therefore get to the rubbish. Constructing a weld-mesh roof, and blocking the gap under the door with a board will resolve the problem.

Foxes have a 'grab and go' philosophy. Anything that smells, even vaguely, of food will be snatched by foxes and taken somewhere quiet for examination and possibly consumption or 'caching'. If you keep finding someone else's rubbish in your garden, for example, chip wrappings, KFC boxes, plastic bags, even used nappies, then it is the fault of the people who have failed to properly dispose of their rubbish – not the foxes! One elderly lady client of mine was extremely upset at finding used nappies in her garden every day. I advised her how to devise a simple one-sided leaflet explaining her problem and asking whoever was irresponsibly failing to properly dispose of their used nappies to 'clean up their act.' She and a friend delivered them to every house in her street and to the houses in the street whose gardens backed onto hers. The problem ceased almost immediately.

Sheds and decking

Most urban foxes are born under garden sheds, summer-houses

and increasingly, under decking. In the autumn and early winter, when humans have virtually abandoned the garden because of the weather, foxes are searching for potential dens around their territory. Most people place their garden sheds right in the rear corner of their garden to maximise space. We tend to leave only a small gap between the shed and the fences – too small for us to walk around the shed, but big enough to enable a fox to get around the back, and dig unseen to get under the shed. The excavated soil may be piled up to a height of a metre or more between the shed and the fence and the householder may not be aware that a pair of foxes have taken up residence until half a dozen cubs are playing in the garden in April.

Ideally a garden shed or summerhouse should be sited in the centre of a concrete or paving slab platform at least 60cms wider all round than the shed. If the building is to go into the corner of the garden, the concrete or paving slab base should abut both the rear and the side fence so that foxes cannot hide behind the shed and dig into the soil. Similarly with decking, there should be a 'path' of paving slabs (or alternatively pegged-down two inch heavy weld-mesh) laid flat on the ground wherever the edge of the decking adjoins soil. This tactic will prevent foxes digging under the shed, as they always start digging at the foot of the shed wall, or the base of the decking board. Where decking adjoins garden fences, it may be wise to invite the neighbours to agree to weld-mesh or paving slabs being laid their side of the fence to prevent foxes digging under the fence AND the decking. Alternatively metal or wooden rods can be hammered into the ground (5cms – 7cms apart) to form an underground 'fence'. If the foxes have already excavated a cavity under the shed it is often simplest to dismantle the shed, expose the 'den', fill in the cavity and replace the shed on a new concrete or paving slab platform.

Decking that utilises planks that are fixed tight up against each other will ensure that the space under the decking is dry, and thus favoured by foxes as a hiding place or breeding den. Planks with gaps between will allow the rain through, but often a small shed, or a covered barbecue or seat is placed on the decking, thus leaving a dry patch under the decking at that point. If foxes have moved in, then provided you can remove the screws – (in my experience usually very difficult) then removing a few planks and leaving the area exposed for a few days will result in the foxes moving out, as well as providing you with the opportunity to clean out any fox 'debris' such as KFC boxes, plastic bags, bones etc.

Foxes under the floor-boards!

On average I deal with at least thirty cases a year of foxes setting up home under the floorboards of houses. The main complaints are the smell, both from the foxes or the rubbish they take in, or the terrible stench of a decomposing fox, the noise from bickering cubs banging around amongst underfloor pipework, dust thrown up through the gaps between floorboards, and (fortunately rarely) flea outbreaks. The access, in most cases, is through missing air-vents, particularly the old Victorian cast-iron grills that get cracked by the frost over the decades and eventually fall out. I have also known cases of small vixens squeezing in through the hole left by a single missing air-brick and giving birth to half a dozen cubs under a kitchen floor.

It should not be necessary to say this to intelligent human beings, but as it happens so often I feel obliged to. *Never block a hole until you are positive that no creature is inside!* The only logical solution to evicting foxes from such accommodation, is to fit a 'one-way gate' over the access hole so that animals can exit, but not get back in. However, this should not be done until it has been established that any cubs present are mature enough to be following their mother on her trips out and back in through the hole. Cubs won't be doing this until they are over a month old, and if it is absolutely vital that the family be evicted before the cubs are that mobile, the only solution is to take up the floor to capture the cubs and place them outside in some sort of shelter, such as a shed or even an open rabbit hutch, where the vixen can choose to keep them or from which she can take them to another den (most vixens have 'emergency dens' in their territory).

A successful design for such a 'one-way gate' consists of a wooden frame, with a hinged flap, ideally with a perspex window so that the foxes can see outside before they push open the flap.

Day 1.   The 'gate' is fixed to wall with screws and left overnight.

Day 2.   The flap should be pulled open and a pile of sand or soil placed inside the flap.

Day 3.   The sand should be checked for any disturbance or footprints that would indicate that not all the animals emerged the first night.

If there is no disturbance it can be assumed that the animals have left and something heavy such as paving slabs or concrete blocks should be used to barricade the flap until a new air-vent grill can be installed. If the sand inside the flap *has* been disturbed again, leave the 'one-way gate' in place for another night. There must be at least 24 hours without disturbance of the sand before assuming all the foxes have left, and even then it is wise to listen for any sounds under the floor that might suggest that there are still foxes there.

Garden lighting and irrigation systems

Juvenile foxes, particularly between June and October, do sometimes dig up buried garden irrigation pipes, and bite them into pieces. No-one really knows why, but in my experience the damage usually seems to occur at the junctions of such pipes. Foxes have fantastic hearing ability and I suspect that the swirl of the water in the junctions convinces them that there is a grub or insect at that spot. They dig at the spot, find the pipe and bite into it. However, foxes also dig up the cables of garden lighting systems and bite them into pieces, and even haul water pumps out of ponds by tugging at the cable with their teeth. This sort of damage can be very expensive – particularly as it may be repeated! My recommendation is that all such pipes and cables should be protected by being run through metal conduit. A less expensive solution is covering pipes and cables with plastic guttering of the sort fitted to sheds. Temporary protection can also be provided by spraying exposed cables and pipes with 'Wash & Get Off' repellent.

Play equipment

Foxes, particularly cubs and juveniles are highly curious and very playful. Childrens' and dogs' toys left out in the garden may well be carried off, chewed up, and finally 'scent-marked'

with urine or faeces. Play equipment such as swings, climbing frames and trampolines are often erected at the end of the garden on a area consisting of wood-chips laid upon plastic membrane. Foxes enjoy bouncing on trampolines as much as children, but they have a habit of chewing the edges. Foxes are always attracted to wood-chips and will dig it frantically, exposing and tearing up the membrane. The 'Scarecrow' or 'Jet-Spray Repeller' devices are the ideal protection systems (see also Ponds). Small toys and balls should be put away in a shed or garage at night or when not in use.

Garden football goals with nets are a real hazard for fox cubs. Every year wildlife rescuers are called out to retrieve cubs hopelessly tangled in the nylon string used for the nets. The cubs may still be alive, but their struggles often result in the cord biting so deeply that the blood circulation has been cut off to limbs, and they cannot be saved. To prevent such tragedies, either remove the nets or hoist them up and fasten them to the bar at night or when not in use.

Pets

Rabbits, guinea-pigs, chickens, and exotic pet birds are all natural prey of foxes. The Animal Welfare Act 2006 makes it a legal obligation for the owner of such animals to protect them from predators as well as other forms of suffering. If therefore, such domestic creatures fall victim to foxes due to being kept in inadequate accommodation or through lack of supervision, criminal prosecution could result, adding shame and financial penalty to the inevitable distress and guilt of the family at losing their pets. The flimsy standard 'pet shop' hutches sold by pet shops are not adequate. The light mesh can be ripped out by foxes, the door catch is usually a simple swivel that any predator can knock aside, and if the pets hide in the 'nest box' section, the plywood is usually far too flimsy to defeat a hungry predator. My personal recommendation is that hutches should be kept close to the house, fixed to a wall at a height of one and half metres, strong enough to withstand a full scale

attack by a large breed of dog, the doors secured with padlocks (to defeat human thieves as well as predators) and ideally, the animals transferred at night to another hutch in a locked shed or garage. Outside hutches and pens can however be defended at night by the 'Scarecrow' or 'Jet-Spray Repeller' devices. (See ponds).

Information on the construction of rabbit hutches as well as general rabbit welfare information can be obtained from the Rabbit Welfare Association (www.rabbitwelfare.co.uk)

Vulnerable pets or poultry should never be allowed to free-range unsupervised in the garden. Even going in to make a cup of tea or being called away to answer the phone may result in tragedy. Remember that although rural foxes are still mostly nocturnal in their lifestyles, urban foxes can be out and about at all times of the day and night. And the local foxes will know of the whereabouts of every rabbit and chicken in their territory.

Cats and foxes normally share territory without serious conflict. Foxes will dig up the bodies of pet cats that have been buried in the garden, and also scavenge the bodies of cats killed on the roads. The fact that a dead cat has been found dismembered by foxes in a garden enclosed by a high fence, does not mean that the cat's death could not have been caused by a road accident. It is a fact that cats when hit by cars, are sometimes capable of leaping a fence and getting into a garden before they die of their injuries. Their bodies may then be scavenged by foxes and everyone assumes the foxes must have killed the cat. I remember as a motorcyclist in my late teens I ran over a cat that leapt out in front of me, and I looked back to see it vanishing over five feet high wall. Despite an extensive search I found no trace of the cat, but I cannot imagine it survived being run over by both wheels of a heavy 500cc Triumph motorcycle plus my 12 stones. Many foxes too, are found dead in fenced gardens having been hit by cars and yet managed to dash away and scramble over high fences before dying of internal injuries.

Foxes know full well that cats are a formidable foe and if attacked by a cat most foxes will turn tail. In my experience some foxes will confront a cat if it approaches too close to their den or young cubs, but this normally only happens in the breeding period of February to the end of May. It seems that this behaviour by the fox is such a surprise to some cats, that instead of fluffing-up and spitting, the cat turns and runs for the cat flap. To a canine like a fox, this is as good as an invitation to chase and I have known a handful of cases where cats have been bitten in the tail or back legs.

I have also known a couple of cases where foxes have attacked cats at other periods of the year, but these have either been kittens or frail, elderly and deaf cats that were not aware of the presence of a fox until it was too late. All cats, but especially very young and very old cats, should be shut in at night and the cat flap locked. It's at night when cats get involved in fights with other cats, at night when they get confused by car headlights, and at night when they might fall victim to the new British bloodsport of yobs hunting cats with lurchers around the street in the middle of the night. When I lived in South East London, there were three cats killed in two weeks in our road in the middle of the night. I saw one of the attacks myself after hearing the dogs in the street. I saw from my bedroom window, two lurchers savage an elderly cat to death in a front garden 40 yards down the road. Apparently, in their ignorance, the police had responded to the first two reports of cats found savaged to death, by suggesting it 'must be foxes'.

Dogs are the evolutionary enemy of foxes, and I have only ever come across a handful of cases of vixens setting up a breeding den in gardens to which a dog had access. One case involved a tiny 'toy' breed which I assume the adult foxes regarded as harmless,. Another case involved a huge, middle-aged Great-Dane cross that completely ignored the foxes and lazily flopped out asleep on the patio, and another involved a case where the owners of the house and their dog had been away for a month. While they were away, the vixen gave birth to cubs under the garden shed. When the family returned the dog was immediately aware of 'squatters' and constantly attempted to get under the shed, until the vixen moved her family away in the middle of the night. So the presence of dogs is probably the most effective fox repellent available. I managed to persuade a vixen in Worthing to move her cubs from her den under a summer-house, simply by walking my dog around the garden to scent mark, and by placing clumps of his groomed-out hair at various points around the garden. That night, my client watched the vixen carry her cubs, one at a time, over the fence and away.

Fox attacks on dogs are very rare, and only ever involve tiny dogs, and are as uncommon as the occasions when a dog and fox strike up a friendship (which has even happened with cats and foxes). In the handful of cases I've known personally, where a fox had attacked a small dog, it has been naive juvenile foxes, and in one case a vixen with cubs.

An issue which annoys me intensely as I know it does with staff of the Fox Project, National Fox Welfare Society and other wildlife groups, is that some vets insist on describing Sarcoptic mange as 'fox mange'. There is no such disease as 'fox mange'. I have consistently used dogs for tracking foxes in London for more than a decade and some of those foxes have been suffering from severe mange – sometimes to the extent that they have been virtually bald and bearing raw patches and scabs. I have had a couple of problems when my dogs have picked up fleas but none of them have ever been been infected with mange mites. Some vets confronted with a skin problem in dogs, put it down to 'fox mange' without even taking the logical step of taking skin scrapings to identify the cause. Although Sarcoptic mange is regarded as highly contagious, one can often find fox families where all but one are in fine condition, while the other is suffering severely from mange. This suggests that the real issue is the level of immunity in individual animals. We have all worked with people who always seem to be catching colds, and others who never catch one. If you have a dog that suffers from a skin disease, don't accept that it has 'fox mange' unless your vet has shown you the evidence that it has been infected by Sarcoptic mange mites.

Cars

Every summer, usually between July and October, I get a handful of calls about foxes jumping on cars, scratching paint-work, biting off aerials, and stripping windscreen wiper blades. This 'vandalism' is the work of 'teenage' juvenile foxes, chasing each other, mock-fighting and playing 'king-of-the castle' on parked cars. Occasionally the damage can be more serious and I have dealt with a few cases of foxes getting underneath cars and biting into brake pipes and electric cables in their excited state. I once had Epsom police visit me to show me pipes and electric wires that appeared to have been neatly cut. They had been staking out a road every night for a week trying to catch what people assumed to be a human with some sort of vendetta against car owners in the street. Several cars had been damaged, but no-one was ever seen. The officers did report back that they had seen foxes in the road, and indeed after examining the 'evidence' I was able to confirm that the foxes were the culprits and advise that the danger period would be brief. Sometimes the damaged cars are in an underground car-park where adult foxes leave their cubs while they go searching for food. They seem to regard undergound car parks

as a sort of 'creche' where cubs can safely be left to play.
If this problem of damage occurs with cars parked on the drive
or on the road outside the house, the simplest solution is to

move the car some way away for a few days. Foxes, being canines, are creatures of habit and simply moving the car temporarily may disrupt the routine. For cars parked in underground car parks there is a device called 'ScatMat' produced in Canada by Contech Electronics Inc. It consists of a plastic mat (there are different sizes) to which is attached a small power-pack, powered by a 9v battery of the type used in smoke alarms. The mat is laid on the car roof , boot or bonnet, and when an animal stands on the mat, it delivers a mild electric shock of about the same intensity as the static charge one can get from touching a metal banister or car door handle. It is enough to deter any animal such as a fox or cat from climbing or sleeping on cars. At the time of writing ScatMat is not available in the UK, but Foxolutions are looking for a source. It is generally regarded as an indoor device for training cats to keep off kitchen work surfaces or tables.

Where foxes cause damage underneath cars it may be worth spraying 'Wash & Get Off' repellent onto the ground all round the perimeter of the car, or obtaining a length of the small, green, plastic covered wire garden fencing used around flower beds and wrapping it all round the base of the car at night to physically prevent animals getting under the vehicle.

Screaming

At various times of the year, urban residents may find themselves being awoken in the middle of the night by foxes screaming in the street or in the their gardens. There are two main seasons when noise can be a problem. In midwinter December/January foxes are mating. Vixens only come into season for a couple of days in the entire year and the dog fox will follow his mate closely to ensure he doesn't miss his chance. Much of the screaming will be the vixen telling him to clear off until she is ready. Once mating has occurred things go quiet again. In the summer months cubs mock-fighting can be noisy (particularly if the weather is warm enough to leave bedroom windows open) and there may also be a noisy period in the autumn when the cubs are coming under pressure from their parents to leave home and find their own way in the world. There is little that can be done about foxes shouting at each other, apart from shutting the windows and wearing earplugs. Like car alarms, noisy parties, police sirens, and a host of other annoying noises, it's one of those things that townies have to put up with.

Finally, it is possible that you may come across a fox problem not covered in this book. If you do, please try either the Fox Project's recorded deterrence help–line Tel; 01892 826222, or one of the consultants listed in the References and Contacts section of this book. We will do our best to help you find a humane solution. There is one final 'top tip' I can offer for anyone attempting to persuade a fox to move its family of cubs out of their property. Take a look around and ensure that the vixen can physically get her cubs away. Foxes don't normally live long enough to become experienced parents, and they sometimes set up 'earths' in the silliest of places, such as gardens surrounded by a two and half metre high brick wall or fence. The adult foxes may just be fit enough to scramble over such a high obstacle, but obviously cubs have no chance of escape unless their mother can climb the wall with a cub in her mouth – one at a time. If the cubs are approaching three months of age they will be too heavy for a normal fox to lift over high walls or fences. Similarly some fences are set on concrete gravel-boards at the base and the foxes cannot dig escape routes under the fences. If you want 'your' foxes to vacate then try to make it easy for them to do so. A plank leaning up to the top of the wall may enable the cubs to follow their mother out of the garden, or creating a 'cat flap-sized' hole in a fence or wooden side gate can provide the foxes with escape routes.

References and Contacts

Contacts

The Fox Project
The Lodge
Kings Toll Road
Pembury
Kent TN2 4BE
01892 824111
Email: fox@foxproject.org.uk
www.foxproject.org.uk

Department for Environment, Food and Rural Affairs
(DEFRA)
Nobel House
17 Smith Square, London SW1P 3JR
08459 335577 (Helpline)
Email: helpline@defra.qsi.gov.uk

Repellent/Deterrent Suppliers

The Fox Shop
0208 226 6293
Email: info@thefoxshop.co.uk
www.thefoxshop.co.uk

Deterrence Consultancy

Fox-a-Gon
41 Northumberland Avenue
London E12 5HD
0208 925 9639 / 07768 903043 / 07973 414935
Email: enquiries@fox-a-gon.co.uk
www.fox-a-gon.co.uk